MOUNT UNION COLLEGE
LIBRARY

WITHDRAWN
UNIV OF MOUNT UNION LIBRARY

D1406596

BIG TRUCKS

written by Mary Gribbin
illustrated by Julian Baker

Ladybird

Words in **bold** are explained
in the glossary.

Copyright © Ladybird Books USA 1996

All rights reserved. No part of this publication may be reproduced or
transmitted in any form or by any means, electronic or mechanical,
including photocopy, recording, or any information storage and
retrieval system now known or to be invented, without permission
in writing from the publisher, except by a reviewer who wishes to
quote brief passages in connection with a review written for
inclusion in a magazine, newspaper, or broadcast.

Originally published in the United Kingdom by
Ladybird Books Ltd © 1995

First American edition by Ladybird Books,
a division of Penguin Books USA Inc.
375 Hudson Street, New York, New York 10014

Printed in the United States
10 9 8 7 6 5 4 3 2 1

ISBN 0-7214-5690-1

BIG TRUCKS

Contents

Dump Truck

Dump trucks deliver sand and gravel to building sites. Their huge, fat tires allow them to travel over bumpy, uneven ground. The driver dumps the sand and gravel out of the truck where the load is needed. The driver then lowers the body of the truck back to its base and drives off to pick up another load.

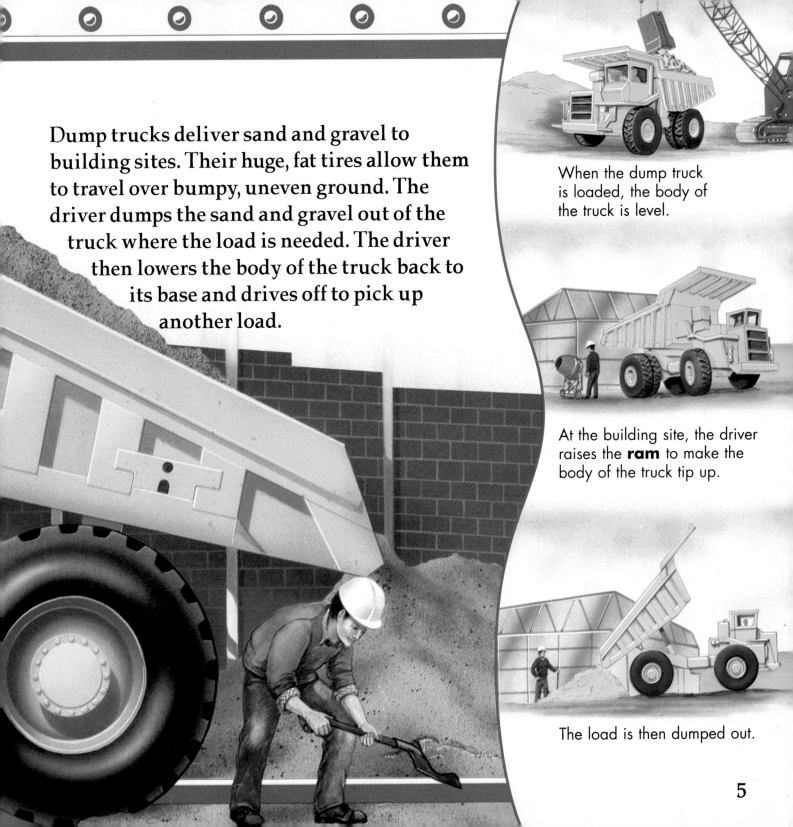

When the dump truck is loaded, the body of the truck is level.

At the building site, the driver raises the **ram** to make the body of the truck tip up.

The load is then dumped out.

The paver spreads tar and gravel over the bumpy road surface.

The steamroller moves slowly over the **blacktop** to flatten it.

Once the blacktop is smooth and hard, cars and trucks can use the road. The new surface will last for many years.

Steamroller

Steamrollers are heavy and slow. They have huge metal rollers instead of tires. The rollers are hollow, but they can be filled with water to make them heavier. Steamrollers are used to build new roads or repair old ones.

Snowplow

Snowplows clear heavy snow off roads in winter. They have big tires with large **treads** so they don't slip and slide on icy streets. Bright headlights help the driver see the road at night or in bad weather.

As the snowplow moves along, the metal blade on the front pushes the snow to the side and clears the road.

Sand or salt is scattered from the back of some snowplows onto the road. This makes the road less slippery for cars.

Tractor Trailer

A forklift is used to load boxes into the back of the trailer.

Tractor trailers take **goods** from one place to another. Large, wide wheels help carry the weight of the load and make the truck safer to drive. The back or the side of the trailer opens up for loading and unloading.

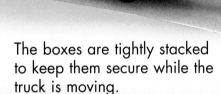

The boxes are tightly stacked to keep them secure while the truck is moving.

The boxes are unloaded at the delivery site.

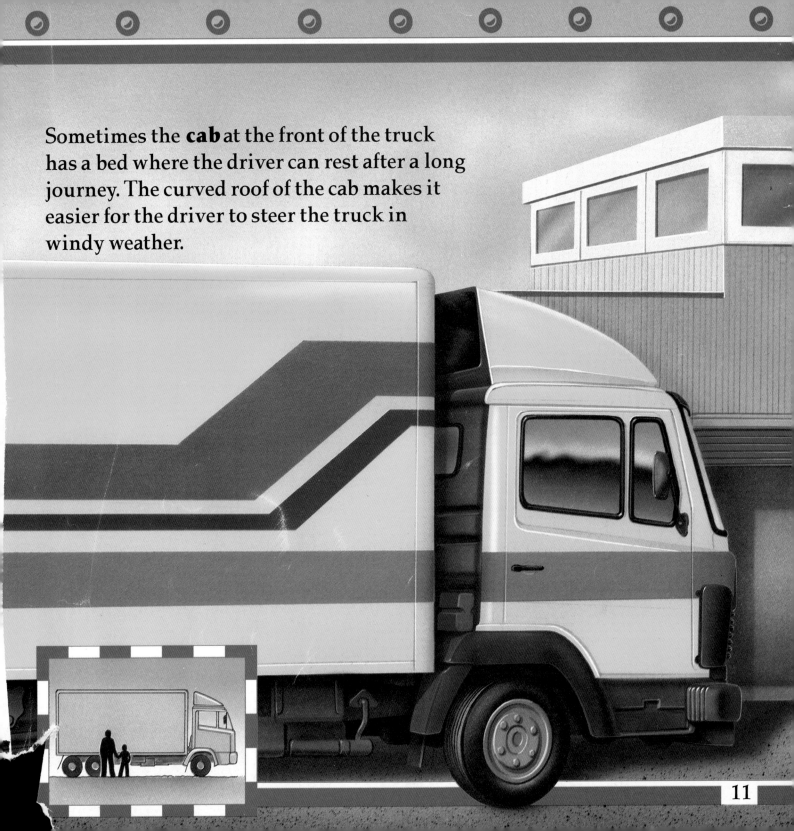

Sometimes the **cab** at the front of the truck has a bed where the driver can rest after a long journey. The curved roof of the cab makes it easier for the driver to steer the truck in windy weather.

Tanker

Tankers transport liquid. Tankers not only carry dangerous **chemicals** but also foods like milk. A long metal tank behind the cab carries the load.

Large rearview mirrors on the sides of the cab help the driver see around the sides of this huge truck. When backing up, the truck makes a beeping sound to warn people to move out of the way.

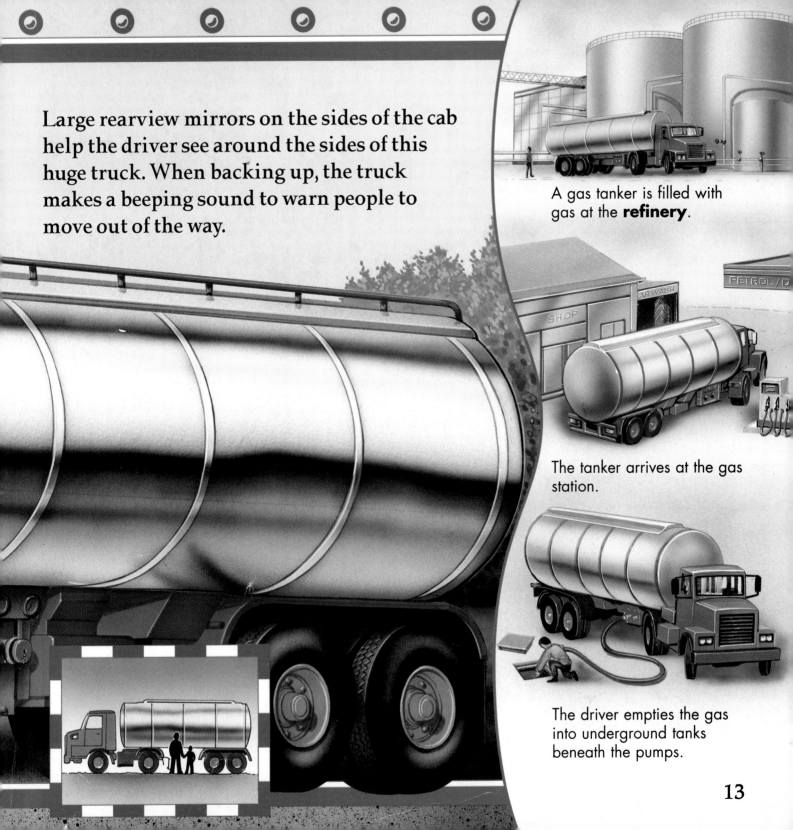

A gas tanker is filled with gas at the **refinery**.

The tanker arrives at the gas station.

The driver empties the gas into underground tanks beneath the pumps.

Car Carrier

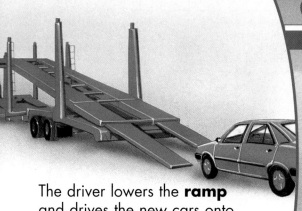

The driver lowers the **ramp** and drives the new cars onto the top deck.

Then the bottom deck is filled. All the cars are tied to the **trailer** with strong **cable** to keep them from rolling off.

At the showroom, a driver carefully backs the cars off the trailer.

Car carriers take new cars from the factory to showrooms to be sold. Most car carriers have more than one deck and can carry up to seven vehicles at once.

Bigfoot Truck

Bigfoot trucks have enormous, tough wheels so they can drive over very rough ground or **obstacles.** Bigfoot trucks are usually only driven in automobile **stunt** shows. All bigfoot trucks have an especially strong frame that protects the driver if the truck crashes or turns over.

Huge tires with thick treads help a bigfoot truck climb over and crush smaller cars.

The bigfoot can be driven on two wheels.

The driver wears a tight seat belt and a helmet for safety.

Tractor

The plow makes **furrows** in the soil.

The spikes on the harrow break up the soil. Then seeds are planted in the furrows.

The crops are sprayed with fertilizer to help them grow.

Farmers use tractors to do heavy work on the farm. Large wheels and rubber tires with deep treads help the tractor drive over muddy, bumpy fields. Tractors pull plows and **harrows** to dig and break up the earth. They also pull seed planters and fertilizer sprayers.

Combine Harvester

Combine harvesters cut crops in the fields. They are very powerful and can harvest huge fields very quickly. The driver sits in the cab, away from the dust and noise. The grain from the crops is made into flour, bread, breakfast cereals, and other products.

The huge reel at the front of the combine harvester cuts the crops.

An **elevator** carries the grain into the threshing drum, where the grain is cut off the stalks.

The grain is dumped out of the combine harvester into a trailer.

21

Fascinating Facts

Dump Truck

Dump trucks that carry heavy loads have extra wheels to keep them from tipping over.

Steamroller

A steamroller can travel only about 6 miles an hour.

Snowplow

Snowplows can be attached to the fronts of trucks and tractors.

Tractor Trailer

Tractor trailers can travel on big ships to transport goods from one country to another.

Tanker

Tankers carrying milk are refrigerated so that the milk stays cool and fresh.

Car Carrier

A double car-carrier can hold up to fourteen cars. The cab can be separated from the car decks and driven on its own.

Bigfoot Truck

The frames of bigfoot trucks are the same size as the frames of ordinary pickup trucks, but they are raised off the ground by big wheels.

Tractor

The first tractor with a gas engine was made in 1892. After that, tractors replaced horses for pulling plows.

Combine Harvester

The combine harvester was invented by Hyram Moore in 1838.

Glossary

Blacktop The dark covering on roads. When the blacktop is hot, it is sticky and has a strong smell.

Cab The front part of a truck where the driver sits.

Cable A thick, strong rope usually made of wire.

Chemical A substance such as gas, oil, or paint.

Elevator A machine that lifts boxes and other goods.

Furrow A long, narrow hole in the ground, made by a plow.

Goods Things people need, including food, clothing, and other items.

Harrow A farm machine with spikes that is pulled by a tractor. The spikes on the harrow break up lumps of soil.

Obstacle Something that obstructs or stands in the way.

Ram The rod that lifts up the body of a dump truck so the load can be dumped out.

Ramp The sloping, back part of a car carrier. Cars drive up the ramp when they are being loaded onto the truck.

Refinery A place where oil is made into gasoline.

Stunt An amazing and sometimes dangerous act that is performed for fun.

Trailer A vehicle that carries goods and is pulled by a car or truck.

Tread The grooves around the outside of a tire. The tread helps a tire grip the road.

Index

Big Giggles

What is a snowplow's favorite Olympic sport?

Truck and field.

What do you call a sleeping Ferdinand?

Bulldozer.

What did the Queen of Hearts scream at the dump truck?

"Off with his headlights!"

Where can you see championship car carriers?

In the Haul of Fame.

How do you get a combine harvester on a roller coaster?

Buy it a ticket.

What is a tractor's favorite magazine?

Truck and Stream.

Where does a bigfoot truck park?

Anywhere it wants to.

What do tankers do when they hear music?

Brakedance.

What is a steamroller's favorite nursery rhyme?

"Pop Goes the Diesel."

What artist do tractors like best?

Toulouse le Truck.

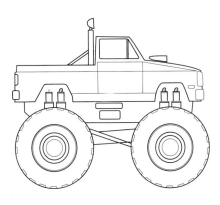

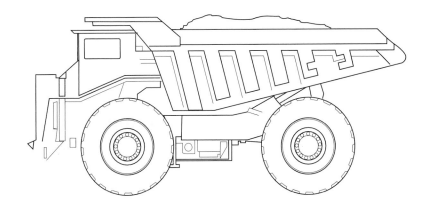

Comparative Sizes

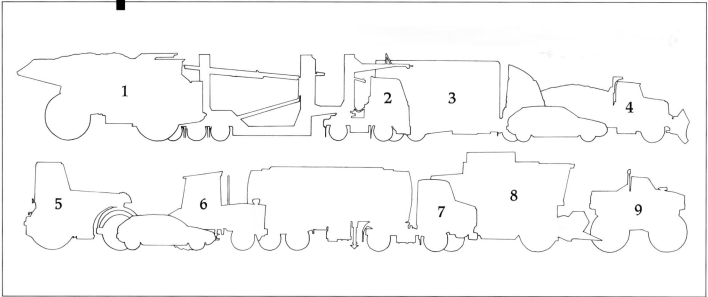

1. Dump Truck

Some dump trucks are so big that the driver has to use a ladder to climb into the cab.

2. Car Carrier

Some of the biggest car carriers can carry up to fourteen cars in a zigzag stack.

3. Tractor Trailer

The biggest tractor trailer carries the space shuttle to its launchpad. The truck moves so slowly that a person can pass it while walking at a normal pace.

4. Snowplow

The biggest snowplow has a 50-foot-wide blade. It was made in 1992 to clear the runway at an airport in New York City.

5. Steamroller

A steamroller can weigh as much as eighteen family cars.

6. Tractor

Some tractor wheels are taller than grown-ups.

7. Tanker

Tankers can hold 9,500 gallons of liquid–enough to fill 1,000 bath tubs.

8. Combine Harvester

In one hour, combine harvesters cut enough wheat to equal the weight of four elephants.

9. Bigfoot Truck

The tracks made by some bigfoot trucks are wider than small cars.

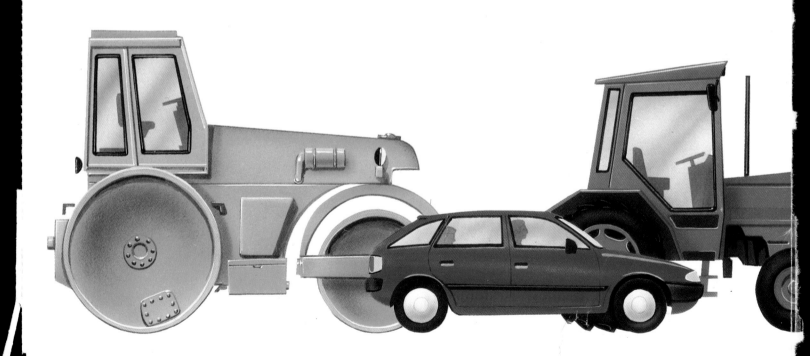